Forward

Welcome to a journey through the timeless myths of ancient Gre
goddesses reign supreme and stories of divine power, love, and tragedy still echo through the ages. In these pages, you will find vivid representations of these iconic figures, each brought to life through a combination of research, imagination, and modern technology.

It is essential to note that all the images you see throughout this book were created by the me using artificial intelligence. These digital creations are not reproductions of real statues or historical depictions of the gods and goddesses. Rather, they are a visual reimagining of ancient myths, brought to life through a modern lens. While the images are inspired by classical art and literature, they are entirely original, crafted using the advanced capabilities of AI image generation.

In addition to the artistic interpretations, all of the factual content within this book has been meticulously researched and fact-checked, drawing from reputable online sources, ancient texts, and scholarly works. The goal has been to ensure that the stories presented here are as accurate as possible, grounded in the rich history and mythology of the ancient world.

As you explore the world of Greek and Roman deities, remember that these images and stories are not only a celebration of ancient traditions but also a testament to the fusion of old and new. Through careful research and cutting-edge technology, these myths have been reimagined and reinterpreted for a new generation to enjoy.

While I have tried to include as many facts as I can, this book is for entertainment only and should not be considered and educational book. I hope you enjoy your journey through the greek and roman mythologies as seen through my eyes.

This stunning depiction represents Aphrodite, the goddess of love, beauty, and desire in Greek mythology, known as Venus in Roman mythology. The artwork captures her divine allure and grace, evoking her central role in mythology as a symbol of passion, fertility, and charm. She is portrayed wearing flowing, elegantly draped garments that emphasize her femininity, adorned with a crown of flowers symbolizing her connection to beauty and nature

This portrayal emphasizes Aphrodite's dual nature—sensual and divine. Her myths remind us of the complexities of love, the interplay of beauty and power, and the enduring fascination with her character in both Greek and Roman cultures.

In Greek mythology, Aphrodite, often called "foam-born" or Anadyomene, is said to have emerged from the sea foam, as recounted in Hesiod's Theogony, following the severing of Uranus' parts and their casting into the sea. Revered as the goddess of love and beauty, she played a pivotal role in mythological narratives, including the Iliad, where her actions in the Judgment of Paris—awarding Paris the golden apple and being deemed the "fairest" goddess—ultimately sparked the Trojan War. Aphrodite was deeply venerated in ancient Greece, with significant cult centers at Cythera, Cyprus, believed to be her birthplace, and Corinth, where grand temples were dedicated to her worship.

In Roman mythology, Venus was revered as the goddess of love, beauty, fertility, and victory, with her iconography closely adopted from the Greek Aphrodite. She was considered an ancestor of the Roman people through her son, Aeneas, the Trojan hero who fled to Italy after Troy's fall, as chronicled in Virgil's Aeneid. Venus held great cultural significance, symbolizing imperial lineage, with Julius Caesar even claiming her as a divine ancestor to legitimize his rule. Romans celebrated Venus through festivals such as Vinalia Rustica and Venus Genetrix, honoring her as the mother of the Roman race and a central figure in their mythology and identity.

Aphrodite and Venus, the Greek and Roman goddesses of love, beauty, and desire, represent the power of attraction and the force of creation in their respective mythologies. Both goddesses share significant similarities, serving as divine figures who embody romance, fertility, and the arts, yet they also reflect unique characteristics and cultural values that distinguish them within Greek and Roman traditions. Their enduring influence extends far beyond ancient mythology, shaping art, literature, and societal ideals of beauty and love even in modern times.

In both Greek and Roman mythology, Aphrodite and Venus are celebrated as goddesses of love and beauty, whose powers transcend both mortals and gods. They are associated with passion, procreation, and the irresistible allure that drives human and divine relationships. Both goddesses are often depicted with symbols of beauty and sensuality, such as roses, doves, and myrtle, and are accompanied by the Erotes (winged gods of love) or Cupid (Eros in Greek mythology). Their myths frequently highlight the transformative power of love and the complexities of desire, underscoring their roles as both creators of harmony and instigators of conflict.

Aphrodite, in Greek mythology, is traditionally described as being born from the sea foam, a dramatic and poetic origin that highlights her connection to the natural world and the mysterious forces of creation. She is closely tied to stories of both love and strife, such as her role in the Judgment of Paris, which led to the Trojan War, and her relationships with gods and mortals, including her marriage to Hephaestus and her passionate affair with Ares. Aphrodite's worship was widespread in ancient Greece, with major sanctuaries at Cythera, Cyprus, and Corinth, where rituals emphasized fertility and the celebration of beauty. Her dual nature as a goddess of both romantic and physical love reflects the Greek view of love as a powerful, multifaceted force.

Venus, the Roman counterpart to Aphrodite, inherited many of her Greek attributes but also took on additional roles that emphasized Roman ideals. While Venus was also a goddess of love and beauty, she was more explicitly tied to fertility, prosperity, and civic order. The Romans revered Venus as a divine ancestor, believing that she was the mother of Aeneas, the Trojan hero who founded the Roman people. This connection made her a symbol of Roman identity and imperial power. Venus's festivals, such as Veneralia, celebrated her as a guardian of love and domestic harmony, while her temples, like the Temple of Venus Genetrix in Rome, underscored her importance to the Roman state and its values of family and lineage.

The influence of Aphrodite and Venus on their respective societies was profound. In ancient Greece, Aphrodite's myths and worship reflected the dual nature of love as both a source of joy and a cause of strife, highlighting the complexities of human relationships. Her association with beauty and fertility reinforced ideals of harmony and prosperity. In Rome, Venus's role as a protector of the state and a symbol of fertility and abundance emphasized the importance of love and family as foundations of society. Her connection to Rome's founding myths also reinforced the legitimacy of the Roman Empire and its divine favor.

In modern times, Aphrodite and Venus continue to be powerful symbols of love, beauty, and desire. Their stories inspire countless works of art, literature, and popular culture, from Renaissance paintings to modern interpretations in film and media. Aphrodite's connection to the complexities of love and relationships resonates in discussions about the nature of attraction and the interplay between passion and conflict. Venus's association with fertility and prosperity influences contemporary depictions of femininity and abundance, often serving as an archetype of grace and allure.

Aphrodite and Venus embody timeless themes of love, beauty, and creation, serving as reminders of the transformative power of attraction and the importance of harmony in both personal and societal relationships. From ancient sanctuaries to modern culture, their legacy continues to inspire and illuminate the human experience, proving that their influence is as enduring as the forces they represent.

This striking portrayal depicts Apollo, the god of music, prophecy, healing, and the sun in both Greek and Roman mythology. The artwork captures his youthful and athletic form, draped in elegant robes and crowned with a laurel wreath, a symbol of victory and his association with the arts. He holds a lyre, signifying his role as the god of music and poetry, with flames in the background symbolizing his connection to the sun and divine power.

Apollo, a prominent Olympian god, was the son of Zeus and Leto, and the twin brother of Artemis. Renowned for his vast range of domains, Apollo was the god of prophecy, music, healing, archery, and the sun. His most revered sanctuary was at Delphi, where the Oracle of Delphi, the Pythia, delivered prophetic insights believed to be directly inspired by him, marking Delphi as the spiritual center of the ancient Greek world. Apollo embodied order, reason, and enlightenment, serving as a symbol of youthful beauty, harmony, and intellectual balance in Greek mythology.

In Roman mythology, Apollo was adopted from Greek traditions without significant alteration to his name or attributes, a rare instance in Roman religion. The Romans revered him primarily as a god of healing and prophecy, especially calling on his aid during plagues and times of crisis. Emperor Augustus held Apollo in particular esteem, aligning himself with the god to highlight his own enlightenment and authority. This connection was symbolized by the construction of the Temple of Apollo Palatinus in Rome. Apollo was also celebrated through festivals like the Ludi Apollinares, established in 212 BCE to seek his favor during the Second Punic War, ensuring his continued prominence in Roman religious life.

Apollo, one of the most revered deities in Greek and Roman mythology, is unique in that he retained his name and many of his attributes across both cultures. As the god of the sun, music, prophecy, healing, and the arts, Apollo represents a harmonious blend of intellect, creativity, and divine power. While the Greek and Roman versions of Apollo share many similarities, there are subtle differences that reflect the cultural priorities and values of each society. His influence on ancient and modern societies is profound, symbolizing enlightenment, balance, and the pursuit of knowledge and beauty.

In both Greek and Roman mythology, Apollo is associated with the sun, light, and truth. He is often depicted as a radiant figure, embodying youth, beauty, and perfection. Apollo's domains include music, poetry, prophecy, medicine, and archery, making him one of the most versatile and celebrated gods. He is frequently accompanied by a lyre, symbolizing his role as the god of music and the arts, and a laurel wreath, which represents victory and honor. As a god of prophecy, he was associated with the Oracle at Delphi, one of the most important religious sites in ancient Greece, where he was believed to communicate divine truths through the Pythia, the priestess of the temple.

In Greek mythology, Apollo is the son of Zeus and Leto and the twin brother of Artemis, the goddess of the hunt and the moon. His myths often emphasize his role as a bringer of order and enlightenment, as well as his capacity for both healing and destruction. For instance, Apollo was said to have defeated the serpent Python to claim Delphi as his sacred site, symbolizing the triumph of order over chaos. He was also known for his relationships with mortals and gods, such as his love for Daphne, who transformed into a laurel tree to escape his pursuit. These stories highlight Apollo's dual nature as both a source of inspiration and a reminder of the complexities of desire and power.

The Roman Apollo, while retaining many of his Greek attributes, was more closely associated with statecraft and the well-being of the Roman Empire. Under the reign of Emperor Augustus, Apollo became a symbol of Roman order, stability, and cultural refinement. Augustus claimed Apollo as his patron deity, aligning himself with the god's attributes of enlightenment and prophecy to reinforce his authority and divine favor. The construction of the Temple of Apollo Palatinus on the Palatine Hill in Rome underscored Apollo's elevated status in Roman society. While the Greek Apollo's mythology often explored themes of individual enlightenment and artistic expression, the Roman Apollo was more closely tied to the collective identity and imperial ambitions of Rome.

The influence of Apollo on both Greek and Roman societies was immense. In Greece, Apollo embodied the ideals of balance, harmony, and intellectual pursuit, inspiring advancements in philosophy, medicine, and the arts. His association with the Oracle at Delphi reinforced the importance of divine guidance in decision-making and governance. In Rome, Apollo's role as a symbol of cultural refinement and imperial power reflected the Roman emphasis on order and civic duty. His festivals, such as the Ludi Apollinares, celebrated his contributions to the prosperity and stability of the state.

In modern times, Apollo continues to be a symbol of light, knowledge, and artistic inspiration. He represents the pursuit of excellence and the harmony between mind and body, influencing fields as diverse as literature, music, and science. The term "Apollonian" is used to describe qualities of order, reason, and clarity, drawing from Apollo's association with these ideals. His image and mythology serve as enduring reminders of the human aspiration for beauty, truth, and enlightenment.

Apollo's legacy bridges the ancient and modern worlds, illustrating the timeless appeal of a deity who embodies both the creative and intellectual forces that define humanity. Whether as the radiant god of the Greeks or the patron of Roman civilization, Apollo remains a powerful symbol of the pursuit of knowledge, artistry, and balance in life.

This is a powerful depiction of Ares, the Greek god of war, presented in a dramatic, heroic pose. He stands tall with a muscular physique, adorned in elaborate golden armor. The armor is intricately detailed, showcasing motifs that symbolize strength and battle, such as a lion's head. He holds a spear in one hand and a large, ornately decorated shield in the other. Ares is also clad in a crimson cape, a color traditionally associated with war, blood, and valor. The fiery background, with flames rising into the sky, emphasizes his destructive and combative nature. The broken pieces of armor and weapons at his feet reinforce his dominance on the battlefield.

In Greek mythology, Ares is the god of war, embodying the brutal and violent aspects of conflict. Unlike Athena, who represents strategic and calculated warfare, Ares is the personification of bloodlust, chaos, and the raw physicality of battle. His primary symbols include the spear, shield, helmet, and occasionally animals like the vulture and dog, both of which are associated with war and death. Ares is the son of Zeus and Hera, but despite his divine lineage, he was often unpopular among the other Olympian gods due to his aggressive and rash nature. In Roman mythology, Ares' counterpart is Mars, a god who was held in much higher esteem and revered as both a protector of Rome and a symbol of disciplined warfare.

In Roman mythology, Mars is more than just the god of war; he is also associated with agriculture and fertility, emphasizing Rome's deep connection to the land and its cultivation. This dual role elevated Mars to one of the most significant deities in the Roman pantheon. While Mars shares symbols with his Greek counterpart Ares, such as the spear and shield, he is also associated with the wolf and woodpecker, both considered sacred animals in Roman lore. Worship of Mars was widespread and profound, with Emperor Augustus dedicating the "Temple of Mars Ultor" (Mars the Avenger) in his honor. Mars was also celebrated during the Roman festivals of March, the month named after him, and October. Unlike Ares, who was often viewed as impulsive and chaotic, Mars embodied discipline and honor, reflecting the Roman ideal of war as a means to secure peace and maintain order.

Ares and Mars, the Greek and Roman gods of war, embody contrasting yet complementary aspects of conflict and power. While both deities share a domain over warfare, they represent very different cultural attitudes toward battle, discipline, and valor. Ares is the Greek god of chaotic and violent warfare, while Mars is the Roman god of strategic war and a symbol of civic duty and agricultural prosperity. These differences highlight the values and priorities of ancient Greece and Rome, and their influence continues to shape modern perceptions of war, power, and masculinity.

In both Greek and Roman mythology, Ares and Mars are associated with battle, bloodshed, and the martial spirit. They are often depicted as powerful warriors, embodying the physical strength and fearsome nature of war. Both gods are accompanied by symbolic figures such as Deimos (Terror) and Phobos (Fear), representing the psychological dimensions of combat. Despite their shared attributes, Ares and Mars were revered in vastly different ways, reflecting the unique cultural landscapes in which they were worshipped.

Ares, the Greek god of war, was the son of Zeus and Hera. Unlike other gods, Ares was often portrayed as impulsive, aggressive, and destructive. His role in Greek mythology emphasized the brutal and chaotic nature of war, earning him both fear and disdain among the gods and mortals alike. Myths involving Ares often depict him as a figure who revels in bloodlust but lacks strategic insight, contrasting sharply with Athena, the goddess of wisdom and strategic warfare. Despite his fearsome reputation, Ares was not widely worshipped in Greece, though he had some cult centers, such as those in Sparta, where martial prowess was celebrated. His myths, such as his infamous affair with Aphrodite, highlight his passionate and tumultuous nature, which further reflects his chaotic personality.

Mars, on the other hand, held a far more revered position in Roman culture. As one of the most important Roman gods, Mars was a symbol of military might, discipline, and civic order. Unlike Ares, Mars was also associated with agriculture, reflecting Rome's emphasis on the dual role of warriors as protectors and providers. Mars was regarded as a father figure, particularly as the divine ancestor of the Roman people through his sons Romulus and Remus, the legendary founders of Rome. This connection made Mars a central figure in Roman identity and statecraft. Festivals such as the Martius (March) celebrations were held in his honor, emphasizing his role in both military campaigns and the renewal of agricultural cycles. Temples dedicated to Mars, such as the Temple of Mars Ultor (Mars the Avenger), underscored his significance as a protector of the state and a symbol of Roman resilience.

The influence of Ares and Mars on their respective societies was profound. In ancient Greece, Ares represented the darker, uncontrolled aspects of war, serving as a reminder of the destructive potential of violence and the importance of tempering aggression with strategy and wisdom. His myths and depictions underscored the Greek ideal of balance in warfare, as embodied by Athena. In Rome, Mars was a unifying figure, embodying the virtues of courage, discipline, and civic responsibility. His dual role as a god of war and agriculture reinforced the Roman belief in the interconnectedness of military strength and societal prosperity.

In modern times, Ares and Mars continue to influence cultural and artistic representations of war and power. Ares is often portrayed in literature and media as a symbol of unbridled aggression and the chaotic nature of conflict, serving as a cautionary figure. Mars, by contrast, is frequently associated with the disciplined and noble aspects of warfare, embodying the virtues of honor and protection. The planet Mars, named after the Roman god, symbolizes strength and determination, further reflecting his enduring legacy.

Ares and Mars represent two sides of the same coin: the destructive and the disciplined aspects of war. Their myths and roles highlight the complexities of conflict and the human experience, offering lessons in the balance between aggression and control. From ancient rituals to modern symbolism, these gods continue to inspire and inform our understanding of power, discipline, and the dual nature of warfare.

This captivating depiction portrays Artemis, the Greek goddess of the hunt, wilderness, and moon, known as Diana in Roman mythology. The artwork embodies her dual nature as a fierce protector of the natural world and a symbol of purity and independence. She is shown with her bow and quiver of arrows, accompanied by a stag, a sacred animal often associated with her, while the forest setting emphasizes her dominion over untamed nature.

Artemis, the daughter of Zeus and Leto and twin sister to Apollo, is revered in Greek mythology as the goddess of the hunt, wilderness, childbirth, and protector of young girls. Known for her fierce independence, she is one of the three virgin goddesses, alongside Athena and Hestia, with her virginity symbolizing her autonomy and refusal to be constrained by traditional roles. Artemis was deeply venerated across the ancient world, with her most famous temple, the Temple of Artemis at Ephesus, celebrated as one of the Seven Wonders of the Ancient World. She is also closely associated with Arcadia and Delos, the latter being her mythological birthplace. Artemis is central to numerous myths, including her protection of her chastity against Orion and Actaeon, who met with her wrath after violating her boundaries, reinforcing her role as a guardian of purity and respect.

Diana, the Roman counterpart to the Greek Artemis, was revered as the goddess of the hunt, the moon, and virginity. She maintained many of her Greek attributes but held a unique place in Roman religion as a protector of women and childbirth. Diana's significance was celebrated in the Festival of Nemoralia, also known as the Festival of Torches, held at Lake Nemi, where devotees honored her under the glow of candlelight. Often associated with lunar imagery, Diana embodied the moon's serene yet powerful nature, symbolizing both tranquility and strength. As a goddess, she represented independence and the harmonious connection between humanity and nature.

Artemis and Diana, the Greek and Roman goddesses of the hunt, wilderness, and the moon, are revered figures who symbolize independence, strength, and the natural world. Though they share many similarities, reflecting their shared mythological origins, they also embody distinct characteristics shaped by the cultural values of ancient Greece and Rome. Both goddesses have left an enduring legacy, influencing not only their respective mythological societies but also modern ideals of empowerment, environmentalism, and feminine strength.

In both Greek and Roman mythology, Artemis and Diana are known as virgin goddesses who protect the natural world and its creatures. They are often depicted with bows and arrows, accompanied by wild animals such as deer, and represent the untamed beauty of the wilderness. Both goddesses are also closely associated with the moon, emphasizing their roles as celestial deities who illuminate the night and guide travelers. As protectors of women and children, they were revered for their association with childbirth and their role as guardians of young girls. Their virginity symbolizes their autonomy and independence, setting them apart from other deities and reinforcing their roles as fierce and self-reliant figures.

Artemis, in Greek mythology, is the daughter of Zeus and Leto and the twin sister of Apollo, the god of the sun. She is often portrayed as a fiercely protective and vengeful goddess, quick to punish those who harm the natural world or violate her sense of justice. Artemis played a significant role in Greek myths, such as her defense of her chastity against Orion and Actaeon, both of whom faced her wrath for disrespecting her boundaries. She was also a goddess of the hunt, revered for her skill and precision. Artemis was worshipped widely across Greece, with major cult centers in Ephesus, where the Temple of Artemis was considered one of the Seven Wonders of the Ancient World, and in Delos, her mythological birthplace.

Diana, her Roman counterpart, retained many of Artemis's attributes but was also deeply integrated into Roman culture and civic life. While Diana was celebrated as a goddess of the hunt and the moon, she was also associated with fertility and agricultural prosperity, reflecting Rome's practical and organized worldview. Diana's worship often emphasized her role as a protector of women and a provider of abundance, aligning her with the Roman values of community and productivity. The Festival of Nemoralia, also known as the Festival of Torches, was held in her honor at Lake Nemi, where worshippers lit candles and made offerings to seek her favor and protection. This festival highlighted Diana's role as a unifying figure in Roman society, connecting individuals with the natural and spiritual worlds.

The influence of Artemis and Diana on their respective societies was profound. In ancient Greece, Artemis symbolized the balance between civilization and the wild, reminding the Greeks of the importance of respecting the natural world. Her myths and worship emphasized the value of independence and the necessity of protecting the vulnerable. In Rome, Diana's role as a goddess of fertility and the hunt reinforced the Roman ideals of prosperity, harmony, and civic responsibility. Her connection to the moon and the cycles of nature mirrored Rome's structured and pragmatic approach to religion and life.

In modern times, Artemis and Diana continue to inspire as icons of feminine empowerment, independence, and environmental stewardship. Artemis is often celebrated in contemporary culture as a symbol of strength and resilience, resonating with movements that advocate for women's autonomy and equality. Diana's association with fertility and the natural world aligns with modern environmental efforts, inspiring conservation and sustainability initiatives. Both goddesses remain central figures in art, literature, and popular media, serving as enduring archetypes of feminine strength and connection to nature.

Artemis and Diana embody timeless themes of independence, protection, and harmony with the natural world. Their myths and roles highlight the importance of respecting boundaries, safeguarding the vulnerable, and embracing the wild and untamed aspects of life. From their revered positions in ancient societies to their lasting influence in modern culture, these goddesses continue to inspire and illuminate the complexities of human and environmental relationships.

The image portrays Athena (Greek mythology), known as Minerva in Roman mythology, depicted in classical artistic style. She is dressed as a warrior goddess, wearing a golden breastplate (the aegis), which is often associated with her protection. A golden helmet with intricate detailing crowns her head, symbolizing her role as a goddess of war and wisdom. Athena holds a spear, showcasing her martial prowess, and a round shield featuring ornate patterns, emphasizing her strategic and defensive aspects in battle.

Athena, the Greek goddess of wisdom, war strategy, and craftsmanship, was uniquely born from the head of Zeus, fully grown and armored, symbolizing her intellect and martial prowess. Unlike Ares, she represents disciplined, tactical warfare and is revered as a protector of cities, particularly Athens, which she won by gifting the olive tree, symbolizing peace and prosperity. Known for her aegis, an armor adorned with Medusa's head, and her owl, a symbol of wisdom, Athena played a vital role in myths, aiding heroes like Odysseus and Perseus. A patroness of the arts and skilled labor, she remained a virgin goddess, embodying independence and control, and was celebrated in grand temples like the Parthenon, a lasting symbol of her legacy.

Minerva, the Roman goddess of wisdom, strategic warfare, and the arts, was one of the most important deities in Roman mythology, revered as part of the Capitoline Triad alongside Jupiter and Juno. Often equated with the Greek goddess Athena, Minerva shared attributes of intelligence, craftsmanship, and protection, but her focus leaned more toward knowledge, invention, and the peaceful pursuits of the arts and sciences. She was considered the patroness of poets, musicians, teachers, and craftsmen, embodying the intellectual and creative spirit of Roman culture. Minerva was associated with the owl, symbolizing wisdom, and her sacred day, the Quinquatria festival, was celebrated annually in March, originally to mark the start of the military campaign season. Unlike her Greek counterpart, Minerva was less involved in direct martial exploits, reflecting Rome's emphasis on governance and order. Her influence extended to various aspects of life, making her a multifaceted goddess revered for her guidance in intellectual, artistic, and strategic endeavors.

Athena and Minerva, the Greek and Roman goddesses of wisdom, warfare, and the arts, embody intelligence, strategy, and civic responsibility. Both goddesses share significant attributes, such as their association with wisdom, their roles as protectors of cities, and their depiction as warrior deities. However, they also reflect the unique cultural ideals and priorities of ancient Greece and Rome. Their influence on mythology and society has endured through the centuries, shaping values, ideals, and symbols in both ancient and modern contexts.

In both Greek and Roman mythology, Athena and Minerva are revered as goddesses of wisdom and strategic warfare. They represent the intellectual and disciplined aspects of conflict, contrasting with the chaotic and violent tendencies of gods like Ares and Mars. Both goddesses are often depicted wearing armor, including a helmet and shield, and carrying a spear. The aegis, a protective cloak adorned with the head of Medusa, is a shared symbol of their divine power and ability to inspire fear in their enemies. They are also patrons of the arts, crafts, and intellectual pursuits, emphasizing their roles as guardians of culture and civilization. Both Athena and Minerva were celebrated for their virginity, which symbolized their independence and devotion to their divine responsibilities.

Athena, in Greek mythology, is the daughter of Zeus and was famously born fully grown and armored from his forehead, symbolizing her role as a goddess of intellect and strategy. She is deeply connected to the city of Athens, which was named in her honor after she gifted the olive tree, a symbol of peace and prosperity, to its people. Athena's myths often highlight her involvement in the lives of heroes, such as Odysseus in the Odyssey, whom she guided with her wisdom, and Perseus, whom she aided in slaying Medusa. Her worship was widespread in ancient Greece, with the Parthenon in Athens serving as her most iconic temple. Athena also represented justice and fairness, often mediating conflicts and emphasizing the importance of rationality over emotion.

Minerva, the Roman counterpart to Athena, retained many of her Greek attributes but was also closely tied to Roman values of discipline, order, and civic duty. Minerva was a central figure in the Capitoline Triad, alongside Jupiter and Juno, reflecting her importance in Roman religion and governance. While Athena's myths often emphasized her role in warfare and heroism, Minerva's domain extended to include practical knowledge and craftsmanship, such as weaving and medicine. Her festivals, such as the Quinquatria, celebrated her as a patroness of the arts and learning, underscoring her role in nurturing Roman cultural and intellectual achievements. Unlike Athena, Minerva's association with war was less pronounced, reflecting the Roman emphasis on strategic statecraft and societal organization.

The influence of Athena and Minerva on their respective societies was profound. In ancient Greece, Athena was a symbol of civic pride and unity, embodying the ideals of democracy, wisdom, and cultural achievement that defined Athenian identity. Her myths and worship inspired advancements in philosophy, art, and architecture, leaving a legacy that continues to shape Western thought. In Rome, Minerva's role as a protector of the state and a patroness of education and crafts reinforced the Roman ideals of discipline, productivity, and civic responsibility. Her temples and festivals celebrated the interconnectedness of intellectual and practical pursuits, reflecting the Roman aspiration for cultural and societal excellence.

In modern times, Athena and Minerva remain enduring symbols of wisdom, strategy, and empowerment. Athena's image is often invoked in discussions of leadership, justice, and the pursuit of knowledge, while Minerva's association with the arts and learning continues to inspire creativity and innovation. Both goddesses serve as archetypes of strong, intelligent, and independent women, resonating with contemporary movements that advocate for gender equality and education. Their legacy is evident in art, literature, and popular culture, where they continue to represent the pursuit of wisdom, the importance of strategy, and the balance between strength and intellect.

Athena and Minerva embody timeless themes of intellect, power, and civic duty. Their myths and roles highlight the importance of wisdom, creativity, and justice in shaping human society. From ancient temples to modern ideals, these goddesses continue to inspire and illuminate the complexities of human experience, proving that their influence is as relevant today as it was in the ancient world.

This image depicts Demeter, the Greek goddess of agriculture, grain, and fertility, beautifully portrayed in a golden wheat field at sunset. She wears a flowing green gown symbolizing growth and abundance, accented by golden details that reflect her connection to the earth's riches. Her head is adorned with a crown of laurel or wheat, emphasizing her role as the bringer of harvest. She carries a basket overflowing with fruits, symbolizing the bounty of the earth and her nurturing influence on humanity. The background features a classical temple, representing the reverence she received in ancient Greek religion.

In Greek mythology, Demeter was the goddess of agriculture, grain, fertility, and the harvest, revered as a motherly figure who sustained humanity through her gifts of food and farming. She is best known for the myth of her daughter, Persephone, who was abducted by Hades to the underworld. In her grief, Demeter caused the earth to become barren, leading to the creation of the seasons: spring and summer marked Persephone's return, while autumn and winter reflected Demeter's sorrow during her absence. Demeter was central to the Eleusinian Mysteries, ancient rites that promised initiates insight into life, death, and rebirth. She was often depicted with symbols such as wheat sheaves, poppies, and a torch, the latter referencing her search for Persephone. Known as a nurturing and protective deity, Demeter also presided over the cycle of life and death, ensuring the fertility of the land and the prosperity of crops. Temples and festivals, like the Thesmophoria, were dedicated to her, celebrating her role in agriculture, motherhood, and human survival. Her enduring legacy highlights her vital place in Greek mythology as a guardian of the earth's sustenance and natural cycles.

In Roman mythology, Ceres, the counterpart of the Greek goddess Demeter, was the goddess of agriculture, grain, fertility, and motherhood, central to Roman life and the natural cycles of growth and harvest. The word "cereal" comes from her name, highlighting her connection to agriculture. Her most famous myth involves her daughter Proserpina (Persephone in Greek mythology), who was abducted by Pluto (Hades). Ceres's grief caused the earth to wither, creating the seasons: her joy at Proserpina's return brought spring and summer, while her absence caused autumn and winter. Ceres was part of the Aventine Triad with Liber and Libera, deities of wine and fertility, and was honored in the Cerealia festival, celebrated with games and offerings of grain. Her symbols include the cornucopia, wheat sheaves, poppies, and torches, reflecting her roles in agriculture and motherhood. As a maternal figure, she embodied the earth's life-giving and nurturing aspects, making her a central figure in Roman religion and society.

Demeter and Ceres, the Greek and Roman goddesses of agriculture and fertility, are central figures in their respective mythologies, symbolizing the life-giving forces of the earth. Both goddesses share significant similarities, such as their roles as guardians of the harvest and their deep connections to the cycles of life, death, and rebirth. However, they also embody unique attributes and cultural contexts that distinguish them within Greek and Roman traditions. Together, their legacies have left a profound impact on ancient societies and continue to resonate in modern times.

In both Greek and Roman mythology, Demeter and Ceres are primarily associated with agriculture, fertility, and the sustenance of life. They were revered as the protectors of crops and the forces behind the changing seasons, ensuring the fertility of the earth and the abundance of the harvest. The story of Demeter and her daughter Persephone (or Proserpina in Roman mythology) is a shared myth that explains the origin of the seasons. In this tale, Persephone is abducted by Hades (Pluto in Roman mythology) to the Underworld, and Demeter's grief causes the earth to wither and become barren. Only when Persephone is allowed to return for part of the year does the earth bloom again, symbolizing the cyclical nature of growth and decay.

Despite these shared themes, Demeter and Ceres have distinct characteristics rooted in their cultural contexts. In Greek mythology, Demeter's story emphasizes her role as a nurturing mother and a deity deeply tied to the natural world. She was worshipped in rural communities and through major festivals like the Eleusinian Mysteries, which celebrated the cycle of life and death and promised initiates a deeper understanding of the afterlife. These mysteries were among the most sacred and secretive rites in ancient Greece, highlighting Demeter's profound spiritual significance.

Ceres, while closely aligned with Demeter, reflected Roman values of practicality and civic order. As part of the Aventine Triad alongside Liber and Libera, Ceres's worship was closely linked to the plebeian class and the grain supply, which was critical to maintaining the stability of the Roman state. Her temples, such as the Temple of Ceres on the Aventine Hill, served as centers for agricultural rites and legal activities related to land and farming. Ceres also played a significant role in Roman religious festivals, such as the Cerealia, which featured games and offerings to ensure a bountiful harvest.

The influence of Demeter and Ceres on their respective mythological societies was profound. Demeter's myths underscored the importance of agriculture to Greek life, and her role in the Eleusinian Mysteries reflected the human desire for understanding and connection to the divine. Her worship fostered a sense of community and reverence for the earth's natural cycles. Ceres's influence on Roman society, on the other hand, extended beyond agriculture to encompass issues of law and governance, reflecting Rome's structured and pragmatic approach to religion. Her association with the grain supply emphasized the importance of food security and the role of the state in ensuring the welfare of its citizens.

In modern times, the legacy of Demeter and Ceres continues to resonate in various ways. They are often seen as symbols of fertility, motherhood, and the interconnectedness of life and nature. Their myths inspire discussions about the balance between humanity and the environment, reminding us of the importance of sustainable agriculture and the stewardship of natural resources. Additionally, the story of Demeter and Persephone serves as a metaphor for loss, renewal, and the enduring bond between mothers and their children, themes that remain relevant across cultures and generations.

Demeter and Ceres embody the timeless connection between humanity and the earth, offering lessons in resilience, renewal, and the cyclical nature of life. Their enduring influence on mythology, religion, and culture highlights their importance as symbols of sustenance, fertility, and the transformative power of nature. From ancient rituals to contemporary reflections on sustainability and growth, their stories continue to inspire and guide, reminding us of the profound relationship between humanity and the natural world.

This is an artistic depiction of Dionysus, known as Bacchus in Roman mythology, the god of wine, festivity, and ecstasy. The image portrays him as a youthful, muscular figure, embodying vitality and abundance. He is shown wearing a wreath of grape leaves and vines around his head, a common symbol of his connection to viticulture and the natural world. A vibrant red draped garment with Greek-style ornamental borders enhances his divine and regal stature. In one hand, he holds a large golden goblet of wine, a clear emblem of his dominion over wine and celebration. In the other, he clutches a bunch of ripe purple grapes, further reinforcing his association with the harvest and revelry.

In Greek mythology, Dionysus was the god of wine, fertility, revelry, theater, and ecstasy, embodying both the joyous and chaotic aspects of life. As the son of Zeus and the mortal Semele, he was born twice: first from his mother, who perished due to Zeus's divine form, and later from Zeus's thigh, where he was carried to term, earning him the title "twice-born." Dionysus was closely associated with the vine, symbolizing his dominion over wine and its dual effects—joy and madness. He was a god of transformation, breaking societal norms through ecstatic rituals and the Dionysian Mysteries, where followers sought liberation from the constraints of ordinary life. Known for his entourage, the Thiasos, which included satyrs, maenads, and the god Pan, Dionysus roamed the world spreading the cultivation of vines. He was also linked to the theater, with the City Dionysia festival in Athens celebrating him through dramatic performances. Symbols of Dionysus include the grapevine, ivy, a thyrsus (a staff wrapped in ivy and topped with a pinecone), and a chariot pulled by leopards. His myths often explore themes of life, death, and rebirth, as seen in his connection to the Orphic mysteries. Dionysus represents both the pleasures and chaos of life, making him one of the most complex and influential gods in Greek mythology.

In Roman mythology, Bacchus, the counterpart of the Greek god Dionysus, was the god of wine, festivity, fertility, and ecstatic revelry. He symbolized the liberating power of wine and its ability to break societal constraints, encouraging freedom of expression and uninhibited celebration. Bacchus was often accompanied by a wild entourage of satyrs, maenads, and his tutor Silenus, embodying the joyous yet chaotic energy he represented. Festivals like the Bacchanalia, initially secretive rites held in his honor, were infamous for their ecstatic and, at times, controversial revelry, leading to eventual restrictions by the Roman Senate. His symbols include the grapevine, ivy, and the thyrsus, a staff adorned with ivy and a pinecone, as well as leopards or panthers, which often pulled his chariot. While associated with pleasure, Bacchus also had a deeper significance, representing the cycles of life, death, and rebirth, as seen in his myths. He was also linked to the theater and the arts, reflecting the creative inspiration wine was thought to provide. Bacchus's worship celebrated both the joyous and transformative aspects of life, making him a central figure in Roman culture and spirituality.

Dionysus and Bacchus, the Greek and Roman gods of wine, revelry, and ecstasy, are vibrant figures in their respective mythologies, representing both the joys and the chaos of life. As deities associated with wine and its transformative powers, they were revered for their ability to bring both pleasure and madness, symbolizing the duality of human experience. While they share significant similarities, Dionysus and Bacchus also reflect the unique cultural values and traditions of ancient Greece and Rome. Their influence on mythological societies and their enduring legacy in modern culture highlight their timeless appeal.

In both Greek and Roman mythology, Dionysus and Bacchus are closely associated with wine, fertility, and the celebration of life. They were worshipped as gods who could dissolve boundaries, whether between mortals and gods or between societal norms and uninhibited freedom. Wine, their sacred element, was seen as a divine gift that could foster communal harmony and joy while also unleashing wild, untamed energies. Both deities were also linked to theater and the arts, inspiring creativity and expression. Their followers, often known as Maenads or Bacchantes, engaged in ecstatic rituals and celebrations that emphasized liberation from the constraints of everyday life.

Despite these shared attributes, Dionysus and Bacchus exhibit unique characteristics shaped by their cultural contexts. In Greek mythology, Dionysus was a complex and multifaceted god. He was the son of Zeus and the mortal Semele, and his birth was marked by tragedy, as his mother perished upon seeing Zeus in his divine form. Dionysus was later raised by nymphs and traveled widely, spreading the cultivation of vines and the knowledge of winemaking. His myths often explore themes of duality, such as life and death, order and chaos, and joy and sorrow. Dionysus was celebrated in the Dionysian Mysteries, secretive rituals that promised spiritual enlightenment and a deeper connection to the divine. He was also central to Greek theater, with the City Dionysia festival in Athens dedicated to dramatic performances in his honor.

In Roman mythology, Bacchus, though derived from Dionysus, was integrated into Roman culture with a focus on civic and social celebrations. The Bacchanalia, festivals held in his honor, were initially wild and ecstatic but later became more regulated due to fears of political subversion. Bacchus's role in Roman society was less associated with spiritual mysteries and more with communal revelry and entertainment. He was a symbol of abundance and leisure, aligning with Rome's values of prosperity and celebration of life's pleasures. Temples and festivals dedicated to Bacchus highlighted his importance in fostering social cohesion and collective joy.

The influence of Dionysus and Bacchus on their respective societies was profound. In ancient Greece, Dionysus represented the balance between civilization and the untamed forces of nature. His association with theater and the arts encouraged the development of dramatic literature, which remains a cornerstone of Western culture. The Dionysian Mysteries also reflected the Greek desire for transcendence and a deeper understanding of existence. In Rome, Bacchus was a unifying figure in social life, embodying the pleasures and abundance of the empire. His festivals and rituals reinforced the importance of leisure and communal celebration in Roman culture.

In modern times, the legacy of Dionysus and Bacchus continues to resonate. They are celebrated as symbols of creativity, liberation, and the pursuit of joy. Dionysus, in particular, is often invoked in discussions of artistic inspiration and the transformative power of the arts. The concept of "Dionysian" energy, coined by philosophers like Friedrich Nietzsche, underscores his influence on modern thought, representing the ecstatic and chaotic aspects of human experience. Bacchus, meanwhile, remains a symbol of festivity and abundance, often associated with the enjoyment of wine and the celebration of life's pleasures.

Dionysus and Bacchus embody the timeless human desire to embrace both the structured and the wild, the sacred and the profane. Their myths and rituals reflect the complexities of existence, offering lessons in balance, transformation, and the celebration of life. From their roles in ancient rituals to their enduring presence in modern culture, these gods continue to inspire and captivate, reminding us of the enduring power of myth to illuminate the human experience.

Hades is portrayed here as a powerful and enigmatic figure standing in a dark, volcanic landscape surrounded by jagged rocks and molten lava. The dramatic lighting casts shadows across his strong, chiseled features, emphasizing his intensity and commanding presence. His black, flowing robes, detailed with intricate gold embellishments, reflect both his role as a sovereign and his connection to the riches of the underworld. His muscular physique, accentuated by the folds of his clothing, exudes strength and authority.

In Greek mythology, Hades was the god of the underworld and ruler of the dead, overseeing the realm that bore his name. As the son of the Titans Cronus and Rhea, and the brother of Zeus and Poseidon, he played a key role in dividing the cosmos, taking dominion over the underworld while his brothers ruled the sky and the sea. Though often associated with death, Hades was not an evil deity but a just and stern ruler who maintained balance in the afterlife. His domain, often called Hades, was a vast and shadowy realm that included the Elysian Fields (for the virtuous), the Asphodel Meadows (for ordinary souls), and Tartarus (for the wicked). Hades was known for his wealth, as all precious metals and gems came from beneath the earth, earning him the title "Plouton" (the wealthy one). His symbols include the Cerberus, his three-headed dog that guarded the gates of the underworld, and the helm of darkness, which rendered him invisible. One of his most famous myths involves the abduction of Persephone, whom he made his queen. Despite his fearsome reputation, Hades was a vital figure in Greek mythology, embodying the inevitability of death and the order of the afterlife.

In Roman mythology, Pluto, the counterpart of the Greek god Hades, was the god of the underworld and ruler of the dead. As a deity, he was also associated with wealth and the riches found beneath the earth, such as precious metals and fertile soil, earning him the title "Dis Pater," meaning "Father of Wealth." Unlike his Greek counterpart, Pluto was often seen in a more neutral or even positive light, emphasizing his role as a provider of abundance and a guardian of order in the afterlife. His domain included all aspects of the underworld, from the Elysian Fields, a paradise for the virtuous, to Tartarus, a place of punishment for the wicked. Pluto's myth of abducting Proserpina (Persephone in Greek mythology) and making her his queen explained the cycle of the seasons, as her time spent in the underworld caused winter while her return to the surface marked spring. His symbols included the bident (a two-pronged scepter), Cerberus, his three-headed guard dog, and the cornucopia, representing the wealth of the earth. Pluto played a crucial role in Roman religion, embodying death's inevitability and the prosperity that comes from the depths of the earth.

Hades and Pluto, the Greek and Roman gods of the underworld, embody the mysteries of death, the afterlife, and the unseen realms beneath the earth. While they share many similarities, such as their dominion over the dead and their association with wealth derived from the earth's resources, they also reflect the distinct cultural perspectives of ancient Greece and Rome. Both gods played crucial roles in their respective mythologies, shaping beliefs about mortality and the afterlife, and their influence continues to resonate in modern culture.

In both Greek and Roman mythology, Hades and Pluto ruled the underworld, where the souls of the deceased resided. They were not considered evil but rather necessary and just rulers of the dead, maintaining the balance between life and death. Their domain was a place of finality, where mortal souls faced judgment and eternity. Both gods were often associated with wealth and abundance, as the underworld was believed to be the source of precious metals, minerals, and fertile soil. This duality of death and prosperity reflects their roles as both somber and generative deities.

Hades, in Greek mythology, was the brother of Zeus and Poseidon and one of the three major Olympian rulers. His myths often emphasize his stoic and impartial nature. Unlike his brothers, Hades rarely left his domain, and his presence was viewed with both fear and reverence. One of the most famous myths involving Hades is the abduction of Persephone, which explains the origin of the seasons. This myth highlights his role not only as a ruler of the dead but also as a key figure in the cycles of life and nature. Despite his fearsome reputation, Hades was not depicted as malevolent; instead, he was a necessary force in maintaining cosmic order.

Pluto, the Roman counterpart to Hades, retained many of the same attributes but was often portrayed with a slightly more positive and practical outlook. Roman culture emphasized Pluto's role as a god of wealth and abundance, focusing on the fertile and generative aspects of his domain. While still the ruler of the underworld, Pluto was more closely tied to agricultural prosperity and the bounties of the earth. This reflects the Roman tendency to integrate deities into civic and agricultural life, aligning Pluto's role with the stability and prosperity of the state. The Romans also adapted Greek myths, such as the story of Persephone (known as Proserpina in Roman mythology), to align with their cultural values and beliefs.

The influence of Hades and Pluto on their respective societies was profound. In ancient Greece, Hades was central to beliefs about the afterlife and the moral consequences of one's actions during life. The Eleusinian Mysteries, sacred rites associated with Demeter and Persephone, offered initiates the promise of understanding and comfort regarding the afterlife, underscoring Hades's importance in Greek spirituality. In Rome, Pluto's association with wealth and the earth reinforced the importance of agriculture and resource management, reflecting Rome's practical and organized worldview. Both gods symbolized the inevitability of death and the importance of respecting the natural cycles of life.

In modern times, Hades and Pluto continue to captivate the imagination as figures of mystery and complexity. Hades, with his impartial and enigmatic nature, often represents themes of justice, mortality, and the unknown. He has been depicted in literature, art, and popular culture as both a fearsome ruler and a misunderstood figure. Similarly, Pluto remains a symbol of hidden wealth and the transformative power of the earth. The planet Pluto, named after the Roman god, reflects his association with the distant and unseen.

Hades and Pluto embody the universal human fascination with death and the afterlife, offering insights into the balance between life's end and its renewal. Their myths and roles remind us of the importance of accepting mortality while appreciating the resources and cycles that sustain life. From ancient rituals to contemporary storytelling, these gods continue to influence how we understand the mysteries of existence and the enduring power of mythology.

Hephaestus is seen working in a fiery forge, with glowing embers and molten metal surrounding him. His powerful build is emphasized by his broad shoulders and muscular arms, reflecting his role as a divine blacksmith. He is clad in a rugged, sleeveless tunic with worn edges, suitable for a labor-intensive environment. Thick leather straps and belts with detailed metallic embellishments hold his tools and gear in place, enhancing his utilitarian aesthetic.

In each hand, he wields intricately designed hammers, the hallmark tools of his craft. The hammers are adorned with ornate patterns, possibly symbolizing the divine nature of his creations. His beard and long hair flow wildly, capturing the intensity of his work and the untamed nature of his element, fire. His expression is focused and resolute, reflecting his dedication to his craft.

The backdrop features towering furnaces and machinery, glowing with fiery orange light, creating an atmosphere of relentless heat and productivity. Sparks fly around the scene, adding a sense of motion and energy, as if Hephaestus is in the midst of forging a masterpiece.

In Greek mythology, Hephaestus was the god of fire, metalworking, craftsmanship, and volcanoes, renowned as the divine blacksmith of the gods. Born to Hera, and sometimes said to be born without a father, Hephaestus was cast from Olympus due to his perceived deformity, making him the only Olympian known for his physical imperfection. Despite his rejection, he became a master craftsman, creating extraordinary works such as Zeus's thunderbolt, Achilles' armor, and the shield of Heracles. Hephaestus also forged the chains that bound Prometheus and the girdle of Aphrodite, his wife, though their marriage was tumultuous due to her infidelity. He resided in volcanic forges, often assisted by the Cyclopes, where he crafted tools, weapons, and automata. Hephaestus was revered for his ingenuity and association with the transformative power of fire, turning raw materials into objects of beauty and utility. Temples dedicated to him, such as the Hephaesteion in Athens, reflected his importance to artisans and craftsmen. His symbols include the hammer, anvil, and tongs, representing his role as the divine artisan who shaped both the tools of gods and the mortal world.

In Roman mythology, Vulcan was the god of fire, metalworking, craftsmanship, and volcanoes, revered as the divine blacksmith and craftsman of the gods. Often equated with the Greek god Hephaestus, Vulcan was associated with the destructive and creative power of fire, embodying both its potential for devastation and its role in forging tools and weapons. His forge was said to be located beneath volcanoes, and the eruptions were thought to signal his labor. Vulcan was a central figure in Roman religion, particularly in his role as a protector against destructive fires, which was celebrated during the Volcanalia, an annual festival held on August 23. During this festival, Romans offered sacrifices, including fish and animals, to appease him and prevent catastrophic fires in their cities. Vulcan was also associated with crafting legendary items for the gods, such as weapons and armor, and was depicted with tools of his trade, including the hammer, anvil, and tongs. His myths include his marriage to Venus (Aphrodite in Greek mythology), which, like his Greek counterpart, was marked by her infidelity. Vulcan's dual nature—destructive yet creative—made him a symbol of both the perils and the transformative power of fire.

Hephaestus and Vulcan, the Greek and Roman gods of fire, craftsmanship, and metallurgy, represent the creative and destructive power of fire and the ingenuity of skilled artisans. Both deities were revered as master smiths, forging weapons, tools, and wonders for gods and mortals alike. Despite their shared attributes, Hephaestus and Vulcan have distinct characteristics and cultural contexts that reflect the values and priorities of ancient Greece and Rome. Their enduring legacy continues to influence modern society as symbols of innovation, resilience, and the transformative power of creation.

In both Greek and Roman mythology, Hephaestus and Vulcan were associated with fire, blacksmithing, and craftsmanship. They were revered as the creators of divine weapons and artifacts, embodying the transformative power of fire and metalworking. Both gods were often depicted as physically imperfect, which set them apart from the traditionally idealized portrayals of other deities. This imperfection, however, emphasized their unique role as creators and innovators, demonstrating that strength and value come from skill and intellect rather than physical appearance. Their forges, located in volcanic regions, symbolized the raw, untamed power of fire and its potential for both creation and destruction.

Hephaestus, the Greek god of fire and craftsmanship, was the son of Zeus and Hera. He is often depicted as a humble and hardworking deity, tirelessly forging weapons and tools for the gods, including Zeus's thunderbolts and Achilles's armor. Hephaestus's myths often explore themes of rejection and resilience, as he was cast out of Olympus due to his physical deformity. Despite his challenges, Hephaestus's ingenuity earned him a respected place among the gods. He was also associated with automation and robotics, creating self-operating machines and golden handmaidens to assist him in his forge. His marriage to Aphrodite, though tumultuous, highlights the complexity of his character and relationships in Greek mythology. Hephaestus was worshipped in major Greek cities, with temples such as the Hephaesteion in Athens serving as a testament to his importance.

Vulcan, the Roman counterpart to Hephaestus, shared many of the same attributes but was also closely tied to Roman values of utility and statecraft. Vulcan's association with fire extended to its destructive aspects, such as volcanic eruptions and wildfires, which the Romans sought to appease through rituals and festivals like the Vulcanalia. While Hephaestus was primarily celebrated for his craftsmanship, Vulcan's worship emphasized his role in protecting the community from the dangers of fire. His temples, such as the Volcanal in Rome, were often located outside city boundaries to prevent fire hazards. Vulcan's connection to Roman military might was also significant, as his forges were believed to produce the weapons and armor that secured Rome's dominance.

The influence of Hephaestus and Vulcan on their respective societies was profound. In ancient Greece, Hephaestus symbolized the power of craftsmanship and innovation, reflecting the Greek admiration for skilled artisans and the transformative potential of human ingenuity. His myths and worship underscored the importance of resilience and creativity in overcoming adversity. In Rome, Vulcan's dual role as a creator and protector highlighted the Roman emphasis on practicality and communal safety. His festivals and rituals reinforced the idea that fire, while dangerous, could be harnessed for the benefit of society.

In modern times, Hephaestus and Vulcan continue to inspire as symbols of creativity, innovation, and the transformative power of technology. Hephaestus's association with robotics and automation has made him a popular figure in discussions of engineering and science, representing the ingenuity that drives technological progress. Vulcan, with his connection to fire and industry, remains a symbol of the power and potential of human innovation. Both gods serve as reminders of the dual nature of creation and destruction, emphasizing the responsibility that comes with wielding great power.

Hephaestus and Vulcan embody the timeless human fascination with fire, craftsmanship, and the potential for transformation. Their myths and roles highlight the importance of skill, resilience, and creativity in shaping the world. From ancient forges to modern innovation, their legacy continues to inspire, reminding us of the enduring power of myth to illuminate the human experience.

This image depicts Hera, the Greek goddess of marriage and queen of the gods (known as Juno in Roman mythology). She stands regally in flowing white and teal robes adorned with gold accents, holding a golden scepter that symbolizes her authority. Her serene yet commanding expression reflects her divine power. A majestic peacock, her sacred symbol, stands by her side, its vibrant plumage emphasizing her beauty and connection to the heavens. The grand architectural backdrop of columns and warm lighting enhances her royal and divine presence.

In Greek mythology, Hera was the queen of the gods, the goddess of marriage, women, childbirth, and family, and the wife of Zeus. As the daughter of the Titans Cronus and Rhea, she was one of the twelve Olympians and was often depicted as regal and majestic, wearing a crown and holding a␣scepter or pomegranate, a symbol of fertility and abundance. Despite her role as the goddess of marriage, Hera's relationship with Zeus was tumultuous due to his frequent infidelities, and she is known for her jealous and vengeful nature, often punishing Zeus's lovers and their offspring, such as Hercules. Hera was also a protector of women in childbirth and was deeply honored in cities like Argos and Samos, where grand temples were built in her name. Her sacred animals included the peacock, representing her beauty and pride, and the cow, symbolizing fertility. She played key roles in many myths, such as orchestrating the events of the Trojan War after Paris chose Aphrodite over her in a beauty contest. Despite her sometimes fearsome reputation, Hera was a powerful and protective goddess, embodying the strength and sanctity of marriage and family.

In Roman mythology, Juno was the queen of the gods and the goddess of marriage, childbirth, women, and family, serving as the counterpart of the Greek goddess Hera. As the wife and sister of Jupiter, Juno held a central place in Roman religion and was a member of the Capitoline Triad, alongside Jupiter and Minerva. She was considered the protector of the Roman state and had many titles reflecting her diverse roles, such as Juno Regina (Queen), Juno Lucina (goddess of childbirth and light), and Juno Moneta (advisor and protector of wealth, which influenced the modern term "money"). Juno was celebrated during numerous festivals, including the Matronalia, which honored her role as the guardian of marriage and motherhood. Her sacred symbols included the peacock, representing beauty and immortality, and the crown, signifying her regal status. Like her Greek counterpart, Juno was often portrayed as proud and vengeful, particularly toward Jupiter's lovers and illegitimate offspring, reflecting her fierce commitment to the sanctity of marriage. She was deeply revered as a protector of women and a symbol of strength, loyalty, and dignity within the family and the Roman state.

Hera and Juno, the Greek and Roman goddesses of marriage, family, and queenship, represent the ideals of loyalty, power, and protection within their respective mythologies. Both goddesses share significant similarities, as they are each portrayed as the wife of the chief deity (Zeus in Greek mythology and Jupiter in Roman mythology) and are revered as the protectors of women, particularly in matters of marriage and childbirth. Despite these shared roles, Hera and Juno exhibit unique characteristics that reflect the cultural values and traditions of ancient Greece and Rome. Their influence on mythology and society remains profound, shaping perceptions of marriage, power, and loyalty in both ancient and modern times.

In both Greek and Roman traditions, Hera and Juno are associated with marriage and the sanctity of family. They were revered as powerful goddesses who upheld the institution of marriage and protected women during childbirth. Their role as the queens of the gods emphasized their authority and influence within the divine hierarchy. Both goddesses were often depicted wearing crowns or diadems and holding symbols of power, such as scepters, to reflect their regal status. They were also known for their fierce jealousy and protective instincts, particularly in myths involving their husbands' infidelities, which highlight their roles as guardians of marital fidelity.

Hera, in Greek mythology, is a complex figure whose myths often emphasize her struggles with Zeus's numerous affairs. While these myths portray her as vengeful and sometimes harsh, they also underscore her power and resilience as a goddess who demanded respect and loyalty. Hera was worshipped extensively across Greece, with major sanctuaries such as the Heraion of Samos and the Heraion of Argos dedicated to her. She was also associated with the cow, symbolizing nurturing and motherhood, and the peacock, representing her beauty and pride. Hera's importance in Greek society was reflected in festivals like the Heraia, which celebrated women's athletic and cultural achievements, emphasizing her role as a protector of women.

Juno, her Roman counterpart, shared many of Hera's attributes but was also deeply integrated into Roman civic and political life. As part of the Capitoline Triad alongside Jupiter and Minerva, Juno's role extended beyond marriage to encompass the protection of the Roman state. She was revered as Juno Moneta, the goddess of warning and protection, and her temple served as a mint, highlighting her association with wealth and state stability. Juno's festivals, such as the Matronalia, celebrated motherhood and women's roles in society, reinforcing her position as a guardian of domestic and societal order. Unlike Hera, Juno was often portrayed with a more balanced temperament, reflecting Roman ideals of pragmatism and civic duty.

The influence of Hera and Juno on their respective societies was significant. In ancient Greece, Hera's myths and worship emphasized the importance of marriage and family as foundational elements of society. Her fierce protection of these institutions reinforced cultural norms and expectations for loyalty and respect within relationships. In Rome, Juno's role extended to the public sphere, where her association with the state underscored the connection between domestic stability and civic prosperity. Her dual roles as a protector of women and a guardian of the state highlighted the interdependence of private and public life in Roman culture.

In modern times, Hera and Juno continue to be recognized as symbols of marriage, loyalty, and feminine strength. They are often invoked in discussions about the complexities of relationships, particularly in navigating themes of power, jealousy, and devotion. Their stories serve as reminders of the challenges and rewards of partnership, as well as the enduring importance of family and community. Hera's association with resilience and Juno's connection to protection and civic order inspire contemporary interpretations of leadership and the balance between personal and societal responsibilities.

Hera and Juno embody the timeless themes of loyalty, power, and the sacred bond of marriage. Their myths and roles reflect the values of their respective cultures while offering universal lessons about the dynamics of relationships and the interplay between personal and communal well-being. From their revered positions in ancient rituals to their lasting influence in modern culture, these goddesses continue to inspire and illuminate the complexities of human experience.

This image depicts Hermes, the Greek god of travel, commerce, communication, and thieves, known as Mercury in Roman mythology. Hermes is portrayed as youthful and athletic, dressed in flowing blue and gold robes. He holds the caduceus, a winged staff entwined with two snakes, symbolizing his role as a messenger of the gods and a guide of souls to the underworld. His expression is calm and confident, reflecting his agility and intelligence. The background features lit torches, enhancing the divine and mysterious ambiance. In Roman mythology, Mercury retained these attributes but was more closely associated with commerce and trade, emphasizing his role as a patron of merchants.

In Greek mythology, Hermes was the god of trade, travelers, communication, herds, thievery, and cunning, as well as the guide of souls to the underworld. Known for his speed and wit, Hermes was the son of Zeus and the nymph Maia, and he served as the messenger of the gods. He was often depicted wearing winged sandals, a winged cap, and carrying a caduceus, a staff entwined with two snakes, symbolizing diplomacy and commerce. Hermes was a trickster from birth, famously stealing Apollo's cattle as a newborn and later winning forgiveness by gifting Apollo the lyre, which he invented. As a protector of travelers and merchants, Hermes was widely venerated for ensuring safe journeys and successful trade. He also served as a psychopomp, guiding souls to the afterlife, and was closely associated with transitions and boundaries, both physical and metaphorical. Known for his cleverness and adaptability, Hermes played a vital role in many myths, often helping heroes like Perseus by providing tools or advice. His versatility and charm made him one of the most dynamic and beloved gods in Greek mythology.

In Roman mythology, Mercury was the god of commerce, communication, travelers, boundaries, and trickery, serving as the Roman counterpart to the Greek god Hermes. Known as the swift and cunning messenger of the gods, Mercury was depicted with winged sandals and a winged cap, symbolizing his speed, and carried a caduceus, a staff entwined with two snakes, which became a symbol of commerce and negotiation. Mercury was revered as a protector of merchants and traders, ensuring successful business ventures, and was also associated with thieves for his cunning and resourcefulness. He acted as a guide for souls traveling to the afterlife, emphasizing his role as a mediator between realms. Festivals like the Mercuralia, held on May 15, honored him with rituals that included sprinkling water on merchants' goods for prosperity. His quick wit and adaptability made him an important figure in Roman religion and culture, embodying the values of communication, commerce, and ingenuity. Mercury's influence extended beyond trade, as he was also a patron of travelers and a symbol of boundaries, both literal and metaphorical, making him one of the most versatile Roman deities.

Hermes and Mercury, the Greek and Roman gods of commerce, communication, and travel, are among the most dynamic and versatile deities in their respective mythologies. Both gods share a wide range of attributes, acting as messengers of the gods and patrons of boundaries, trade, and invention. Despite their shared characteristics, Hermes and Mercury embody unique qualities that reflect the cultural values and priorities of ancient Greece and Rome. Their influence has endured through the ages, shaping both ancient societies and modern perceptions of communication, commerce, and adaptability.

In both Greek and Roman mythology, Hermes and Mercury are primarily known as divine messengers, tasked with carrying messages between the gods and mortals. They are associated with speed, depicted with winged sandals or a winged cap, emphasizing their ability to travel swiftly across realms. Both gods are patrons of trade, thieves, and travelers, symbolizing the movement of goods, ideas, and people. They are also connected to boundaries and transitions, acting as guides for souls to the afterlife. As tricksters, they are celebrated for their wit, cunning, and ability to navigate complex situations, often outsmarting both gods and mortals.

Hermes, in Greek mythology, is the son of Zeus and Maia, one of the Pleiades. From his infancy, Hermes displayed remarkable ingenuity, famously inventing the lyre by using a tortoise shell and stealing Apollo's cattle as a playful trick. His dual nature as both a mischievous trickster and a benevolent guide highlights his versatility and adaptability. Hermes was revered as the god of communication, eloquence, and invention, playing a significant role in Greek culture. He was also associated with athleticism and was considered a protector of athletes and sports. Temples and statues dedicated to Hermes, such as the herms placed at boundaries and crossroads, emphasized his role in protecting and facilitating movement and communication.

Mercury, the Roman counterpart to Hermes, retained many of the same attributes but was more explicitly tied to commerce and economic prosperity. As a god of trade and financial gain, Mercury was deeply integrated into Roman society, reflecting Rome's emphasis on commerce and expansion. His name is derived from the Latin word "merx," meaning merchandise, underscoring his connection to trade and business. Mercury's festivals, such as the Mercuralia, were celebrated by merchants seeking his favor and protection. Unlike Hermes, Mercury's role in guiding souls to the afterlife was less emphasized, and his portrayal in Roman mythology focused more on his practical and civic importance.

The influence of Hermes and Mercury on their respective societies was profound. In ancient Greece, Hermes symbolized the importance of communication, ingenuity, and adaptability, values that were integral to Greek culture. His role as a guide and protector of travelers reflected the interconnected nature of the Greek world, where trade and cultural exchange flourished. In Rome, Mercury's association with commerce and wealth reinforced the empire's emphasis on economic growth and the movement of goods across its vast territories. His patronage of merchants and traders underscored the critical role of commerce in Roman society and its influence on the development of infrastructure and trade networks.

In modern times, Hermes and Mercury continue to be celebrated as symbols of communication, adaptability, and innovation. Hermes's image is often associated with the swift transmission of information, making him a fitting symbol for industries such as media, transportation, and technology. Mercury's name endures in modern language, from the word "mercurial," describing someone quick-witted and changeable, to the planet Mercury, named for his speed and proximity to the sun. Both gods inspire contemporary interpretations of leadership, ingenuity, and the ability to navigate complex and dynamic environments.

Hermes and Mercury embody the timeless themes of movement, exchange, and transformation. Their myths and roles highlight the importance of adaptability and ingenuity in overcoming challenges and fostering connections. From their revered positions in ancient societies to their enduring relevance in modern culture, these gods continue to inspire and illuminate the complexities of human experience.

Hestia is shown kneeling beside a glowing hearth, the fire's warmth and light symbolizing her dominion over the sacred flame that was central to both Greek and Roman households and temples. Her gentle expression and poised demeanor reflect her role as a unifying and harmonious force among the gods and mortals. The background features architectural columns with intricate patterns, evoking the timeless sanctity of temples dedicated to her worship.

In Greek mythology, Hestia was the goddess of the hearth, home, and family, representing domestic harmony and the sacred fire that sustained communal and household life. She was the eldest child of the Titans Cronus and Rhea and one of the twelve Olympians, though she later relinquished her seat on Mount Olympus to Dionysus to maintain peace. Hestia was a virgin goddess, embodying purity and stability, and was revered in both public and private worship. Every home had a hearth dedicated to her, and the eternal flame in city-state temples symbolized her unifying presence. Newborns were carried around the hearth in a ritual to introduce them into the household, and offerings to Hestia often marked the beginning and end of religious ceremonies. Unlike many gods, she avoided conflict and intrigue, focusing instead on the well-being of the family and community. Her symbols include the hearth fire and kettles, reflecting her role as the nurturing and protective force of the home. Though less involved in myths, Hestia's quiet and constant presence made her one of the most important and revered deities in Greek religion, embodying the stability and warmth of the home and community.

In Roman mythology, Vesta was the goddess of the hearth, home, and family, embodying the sacred flame that symbolized the heart of domestic and communal life. As one of the most revered deities in Roman religion, Vesta was worshipped in both private households and public temples. Her most important temple in Rome housed the eternal flame, maintained by the Vestal Virgins, a group of priestesses dedicated to her service. The Vestal Virgins were tasked with ensuring the flame never extinguished, as it symbolized the safety and prosperity of the Roman state. Vesta's worship was central to Roman life, and her presence was felt in rituals involving the hearth and in state ceremonies, particularly during the Vestalia, an annual festival in her honor. She was a virgin goddess, representing purity, stability, and the continuity of Roman society. Unlike many other deities, Vesta had no personal myths or scandals, focusing instead on her role as a protector of family and community harmony. Her symbols include the hearth fire and the donkey, the latter associated with her sacred rituals. Vesta's quiet yet essential role made her one of the most enduring figures in Roman religion, embodying the unifying power of home and tradition.

Hestia and Vesta, the Greek and Roman goddesses of the hearth, home, and family, represent the foundational values of stability, unity, and sacred tradition. Both deities were central to their respective cultures, embodying the warmth and security of the home and the continuity of communal life. While they share many similarities, reflecting their shared origins, they also reflect the unique cultural priorities of ancient Greece and Rome. Their influence extends from the religious and social practices of their time to modern ideas about family, community, and domestic harmony.

In both Greek and Roman mythology, Hestia and Vesta are associated with the hearth, which was seen as the center of both the home and society. The hearth's fire symbolized warmth, protection, and the unbroken continuity of life. Both goddesses were considered virgins, signifying their purity and devotion to their roles as guardians of the domestic and communal spheres. They were also worshipped through sacred fires that were never allowed to extinguish, symbolizing eternal life and the enduring strength of the community. Hestia and Vesta were both seen as non-confrontational deities, embodying peace, stability, and a harmonious presence that unified families and societies.

Hestia, in Greek mythology, is the daughter of Cronus and Rhea and the eldest of the Olympian gods. She is often depicted as a calm and modest figure, embodying the values of domestic order and hospitality. Hestia was unique among the Olympians in her preference for the quiet sanctity of the home over the dramatic conflicts and adventures of the other gods. She relinquished her seat among the Olympian Twelve to Dionysus in order to maintain peace, further reflecting her commitment to harmony. Hestia was worshipped in both private homes and public hearths, and her presence was invoked during meals and important family gatherings. Despite her lack of dramatic myths, her role as a stabilizing and nurturing force made her an essential figure in Greek culture.

Vesta, the Roman counterpart to Hestia, held an even more prominent role in Roman religion and civic life. As the goddess of the hearth, Vesta was closely tied to the well-being of the Roman state. Her temple in the Roman Forum housed the sacred fire of Rome, tended by the Vestal Virgins, an elite group of priestesses chosen to serve for thirty years. The Vestal Virgins were responsible for maintaining the eternal flame, a symbol of Rome's endurance and prosperity. Vesta's festivals, such as the Vestalia, celebrated her importance to both the state and the family, with rituals emphasizing cleanliness, purity, and domestic order. Unlike Hestia, Vesta's worship was more institutionalized, reflecting Rome's structured and state-centered approach to religion.

The influence of Hestia and Vesta on their respective societies was profound. In Greece, Hestia's presence in both public and private life underscored the importance of the home and hospitality in maintaining social bonds. Her quiet, stabilizing role reflected the Greek ideal of balance and harmony in all aspects of life. In Rome, Vesta's role as a protector of the state and its people reinforced the Roman values of discipline, duty, and communal unity. The Vestal Virgins and their dedication to Vesta's flame became a powerful symbol of Rome's strength and longevity, demonstrating the connection between religious devotion and civic stability.

In modern times, Hestia and Vesta continue to be symbols of home, family, and unity. They inspire contemporary discussions about the importance of domestic harmony and the role of tradition in creating stable communities. Hestia's emphasis on hospitality and nurturing reminds us of the significance of kindness and generosity in personal relationships. Vesta's legacy of communal responsibility and devotion to the greater good resonates in modern ideals of civic duty and collective care.

Hestia and Vesta embody timeless values of peace, stability, and the sacredness of home. Their myths and roles highlight the importance of unity and continuity in both private and public life. From ancient hearths to modern interpretations, these goddesses continue to inspire, reminding us of the enduring power of tradition and the centrality of the home in human experience.

Persephone is depicted standing gracefully amidst a lush and vibrant forest. She wears a flowing golden gown with intricate drapery that symbolizes her elegance and divine status. Her attire is adorned with delicate patterns and golden accents, emphasizing her connection to fertility and prosperity. A crown of roses and greenery sits atop her head, symbolizing spring and life's renewal.

In her right hand, she holds a bright red pomegranate, a symbol of her bond to the underworld. According to Greek mythology, consuming its seeds bound her to Hades for part of the year. In her left hand, she holds a golden stalk of wheat, representing her role as a goddess of agriculture and fertility, closely tied to her mother, Demeter.

The background features blooming roses and a glowing, ethereal light that radiates around her, emphasizing her divinity. Coiled in the shadows is a serpent, a symbol often associated with mystery, rebirth, and the cycle of life and death. The forest setting reinforces her connection to nature and her role as a goddess of spring.

In Greek mythology, Persephone was the goddess of spring, vegetation, and the queen of the underworld. She was the daughter of Demeter, goddess of agriculture, and Zeus, ruler of the gods. Persephone is most famous for her abduction by Hades, the god of the underworld, who took her to be his wife. Her mother, stricken with grief, caused the earth to become barren, leading to the mythological explanation of the seasons. After an agreement was reached, Persephone would spend part of the year in the underworld (autumn and winter) and the other part on earth with her mother (spring and summer), symbolizing the cycle of growth and dormancy in nature. Persephone was both a symbol of life's renewal and the inevitability of death, embodying duality as both a nurturing goddess of life and a regal, powerful queen of the dead. She was closely associated with the pomegranate, which she ate in the underworld, binding her to Hades, and with symbols of springtime, such as flowers. Worship of Persephone was central to the Eleusinian Mysteries, a secretive set of rituals promising spiritual renewal and insights into the afterlife. Persephone's mythology reflects themes of transformation, balance, and the eternal cycle of life and death.

In Roman mythology, Proserpina was the goddess of springtime and the queen of the underworld, serving as the counterpart to the Greek goddess Persephone. She was the daughter of Ceres, the goddess of agriculture, and Jupiter, the king of the gods. Proserpina is most well-known for the myth of her abduction by Pluto (Hades in Greek mythology), who took her to the underworld to be his wife. Her grief-stricken mother, Ceres, caused the earth's crops to wither and die, leading to famine. To resolve the crisis, Jupiter decreed that Proserpina would split her time between the underworld and the surface: living with Pluto for part of the year (autumn and winter) and with Ceres for the other part (spring and summer), symbolizing the seasonal cycle of growth and harvest. During her time in the underworld, Proserpina ate pomegranate seeds, binding her to Pluto and sealing her dual existence as both goddess of renewal and ruler of the dead. Worship of Proserpina was intertwined with the rites of Ceres, particularly in agricultural festivals. Proserpina's symbolism as a bridge between life and death reflects themes of transformation, balance, and the cycles of nature, making her a central figure in Roman mythology and spirituality.

Persephone and Proserpina, the Greek and Roman goddesses of the underworld and springtime, embody the dualities of life and death, renewal and decay, and innocence and transformation. Both goddesses share the central myth of being abducted by the ruler of the underworld (Hades in Greek mythology and Pluto in Roman mythology), which profoundly shaped their roles as figures of rebirth and seasonal cycles. While their stories and symbolism overlap significantly, Persephone and Proserpina also reflect the unique cultural contexts of Greece and Rome. Their enduring influence can be seen in ancient religious practices and modern interpretations of nature, transformation, and feminine resilience.

In both mythologies, Persephone and Proserpina are portrayed as beautiful and youthful goddesses whose lives change irrevocably when they are taken to the underworld. Their shared myth explains the origins of the seasons: as Persephone or Proserpina spends part of the year in the underworld, her mother (Demeter in Greek mythology and Ceres in Roman mythology) grieves, causing the earth to become barren. When she returns, the earth flourishes with growth and renewal, symbolizing the spring and summer months. This cyclical descent and return highlight their roles as mediators between life and death, as well as their connection to fertility and agriculture. Both goddesses became central figures in rituals and mysteries, particularly those focusing on the afterlife and the promise of rebirth.

Persephone, in Greek mythology, is the daughter of Zeus and Demeter. Her abduction by Hades and her eventual role as queen of the underworld mark her transformation from a maiden associated with innocence to a powerful and regal figure. Persephone's dual identity as both a goddess of spring and the underworld reflects the Greek view of life's inherent balance between joy and sorrow. She is often depicted holding pomegranates, a symbol of her connection to the underworld and her binding agreement with Hades. Persephone's worship was deeply tied to the Eleusinian Mysteries, secretive rites that promised initiates knowledge of the afterlife and a deeper understanding of the cycles of life and death. Her myths emphasize themes of transformation, resilience, and the inevitability of change.

Proserpina, her Roman counterpart, shares much of Persephone's story but is more closely aligned with the Roman ideals of family and statehood. While her abduction and eventual reconciliation with Pluto mirror the Greek myth, Roman interpretations often emphasized Proserpina's role in maintaining the balance of the natural world and the prosperity of the Roman state. Proserpina was celebrated during festivals such as the Cerealia, which honored her mother, Ceres, and highlighted their connection to agriculture and fertility. Unlike Persephone, Proserpina's mythology was more integrated into Roman state religion, reflecting the Roman tendency to align deities with civic and agricultural stability.

The influence of Persephone and Proserpina on their respective societies was profound. In ancient Greece, Persephone's story served as a powerful allegory for the cycles of life and the human experience of loss and renewal. Her worship reinforced the importance of agriculture and fertility, as well as the hope for rebirth in the afterlife. In Rome, Proserpina's association with Ceres and the natural world underscored the interconnectedness of family, fertility, and state stability. Her myth reflected Roman values of duty and harmony, aligning with the practical and structured nature of Roman religion.

In modern times, Persephone and Proserpina remain enduring symbols of transformation, resilience, and the cycles of nature. Persephone's journey to the underworld and back has inspired countless works of art, literature, and psychological interpretations, particularly as a metaphor for personal growth and the balance of light and darkness within the human experience. Proserpina's connection to fertility and the changing seasons continues to resonate in discussions about environmental preservation and the interconnectedness of humanity and nature.

Persephone and Proserpina embody the timeless themes of life, death, and renewal, reminding us of the cyclical nature of existence and the transformative power of change. Their myths and roles highlight the importance of balance and resilience, offering lessons that remain relevant in both ancient and modern contexts. From sacred rituals to contemporary interpretations, these goddesses continue to inspire and illuminate the complexities of life and nature.

Poseidon is shown as a muscular and regal deity, his long, flowing silver hair and beard symbolizing his timeless and godly presence. He wields a golden trident, his signature weapon and symbol of authority over the oceans and its creatures. His attire is a flowing sea-green chiton, pinned with an ornate golden brooch, reflecting his divine and majestic status. His waist is adorned with a golden belt intricately engraved with marine motifs, further emphasizing his bond with the sea.

He stands amidst crashing waves and foamy surf, surrounded by vibrant marine life, including dolphins leaping joyfully and colorful coral reefs at his feet. The sunlight beams down through the clouds, illuminating Poseidon and casting an ethereal glow, symbolizing his divine nature. In the background, a chariot drawn by sea horses (hippocampi) rises from the water, alluding to his mythical ability to travel across the ocean with ease.

In Greek mythology, Poseidon was the god of the sea, earthquakes, storms, and horses, and one of the twelve Olympian deities. The son of the Titans Cronus and Rhea, and brother to Zeus and Hades, Poseidon ruled over the oceans and all bodies of water, wielding a trident as his signature weapon, capable of stirring waves or causing earthquakes. Known for his volatile and powerful nature, Poseidon was both revered and feared for his control over the seas, upon which ancient Greek life heavily depended for travel, trade, and sustenance. He was also associated with horses, credited with creating them and often depicted driving a chariot pulled by hippocampi (sea horses). Poseidon's temperament mirrored the unpredictable nature of the ocean, and he often clashed with other gods and mortals; for instance, he contested with Athena for the patronage of Athens, offering a saltwater spring but losing to her gift of the olive tree. Poseidon fathered numerous offspring, both mortal and divine, including the hero Theseus and the cyclops Polyphemus. His symbols, the trident, dolphins, and horses, reflected his dominion over both the sea and land. Poseidon's duality as a giver of life and a bringer of destruction underscored his importance in Greek mythology as a powerful yet unpredictable force of nature.

In Roman mythology, Neptune was the god of the sea, freshwater, and horses, serving as the counterpart to the Greek god Poseidon. As one of the twelve major Roman deities, Neptune was the brother of Jupiter and Pluto, with the three dividing the cosmos among themselves. Neptune ruled over all bodies of water and was revered as a protector of sailors and maritime ventures, critical in a society that relied heavily on the seas for trade and expansion. He was also associated with horses and was credited with their creation, often depicted driving a chariot pulled by hippocampi (mythical sea horses) or regular horses, which tied him to equestrian events and fertility. Neptune was honored during the Neptunalia, a summer festival celebrated on July 23, during which Romans prayed for water during the dry season and held rituals near rivers and springs. His symbols include the trident, dolphins, and horses, all of which highlighted his dominion over the seas and his connection to power and movement. Neptune's mythology emphasizes his dual nature as both a life-sustaining god of water and a force capable of unleashing storms and floods, reflecting his importance in Roman religion and daily life.

Poseidon and Neptune, the Greek and Roman gods of the sea, represent the power and unpredictability of water, as well as its crucial role in life and civilization. Both deities are revered as masters of the ocean and its creatures, with their influence extending to earthquakes and storms. While Poseidon and Neptune share many attributes and domains, their unique characteristics reflect the cultural priorities and values of ancient Greece and Rome. These gods left a profound impact on their respective mythologies and continue to inspire modern interpretations of power, nature, and maritime exploration.

In both Greek and Roman mythology, Poseidon and Neptune are associated with the sea, horses, and earthquakes. They are often depicted wielding a trident, a three-pronged weapon that symbolizes their dominion over the waters. Both gods are seen as temperamental and powerful, capable of causing great destruction through storms and quakes, yet also providing bounty and prosperity through calm seas and fertile land. They were honored by sailors, fishermen, and those whose livelihoods depended on the sea, as well as by communities that valued their connection to horses and chariot racing.

Poseidon, in Greek mythology, is one of the twelve Olympian gods and the brother of Zeus and Hades. Known as the "Earth-Shaker" for his ability to cause earthquakes, Poseidon's temperamental nature is a recurring theme in Greek myths. His disputes with other gods and mortals often highlight his pride and volatile personality, such as his rivalry with Athena over the patronage of Athens, which he lost after offering the city a saltwater spring. Despite his fiery temper, Poseidon was revered as a protector of seafarers and a provider of freshwater springs. He played a significant role in many Greek myths, including the Odyssey, where his wrath against Odysseus for blinding his son Polyphemus shaped much of the hero's journey. Poseidon's worship was widespread in coastal cities like Corinth and on islands such as Delos, where temples and festivals celebrated his power and generosity.

Neptune, the Roman counterpart to Poseidon, retained many of the same attributes but was more closely tied to Roman values of order and expansion. Neptune was not only a god of the sea but also associated with fresh water and irrigation, reflecting Rome's emphasis on engineering and agriculture. His connection to horses was celebrated during the Neptunalia, a festival held in his honor, which emphasized relaxation and the conservation of water resources during the dry summer months. Unlike Poseidon, Neptune was less involved in dramatic myths and was more integrated into Roman state religion, symbolizing Rome's mastery over the seas and its ambitions of maritime dominance. Temples dedicated to Neptune, such as the Basilica Neptuni in Rome, underscored his importance to Roman society and its reliance on naval power.

The influence of Poseidon and Neptune on their respective societies was significant. In Greece, Poseidon symbolized the duality of the sea as both a source of life and a force of destruction. His myths and worship reflected the Greek understanding of nature's power and the need to respect and appease it. In Rome, Neptune's role as a god of both the sea and fresh water reinforced the Roman values of practicality and resource management. His association with horses and chariot races also tied him to public entertainment and civic pride, reflecting the Roman emphasis on community and spectacle.

In modern times, Poseidon and Neptune continue to be symbols of the sea and its mysteries. Poseidon's image often appears in literature, art, and popular culture as a representation of the ocean's vastness and unpredictability, while Neptune is frequently associated with maritime exploration and engineering. The planet Neptune, named after the Roman god, reflects humanity's fascination with the unknown and the drive to explore uncharted territories.

Poseidon and Neptune embody timeless themes of power, nature, and human resilience. Their myths and roles highlight the importance of understanding and respecting the forces of nature, as well as the human desire to harness and coexist with these forces. From ancient rituals to modern interpretations, these gods continue to inspire and illuminate the enduring connection between humanity and the sea.

Zeus is depicted as a tall and commanding figure standing amidst a mountainous landscape, with Mount Olympus in the background, symbolizing his divine throne. His flowing white robes are intricately draped, highlighting his regal and godly stature. Gold accents, including a detailed belt and arm bracers, emphasize his role as a ruler of the gods. His long white hair and beard flow majestically in the wind, underscoring his wisdom and timelessness.

In his right hand, he wields a bolt of lightning, crackling with energy, symbolizing his dominion over thunder and storms. The lightning is vibrant, casting an otherworldly glow around him. His left hand is outstretched, radiating power and authority. A golden eagle soars nearby, a sacred symbol of Zeus, representing his role as the god of the sky and a messenger of his will.

The background features dramatic skies with glowing clouds pierced by sunlight, emphasizing Zeus's celestial domain. The rugged mountain and lush greenery below signify his connection to both the heavens and the earth.

In Greek mythology, Zeus was the king of the gods and ruler of the sky, thunder, and lightning. The youngest son of the Titans Cronus and Rhea, he escaped being swallowed by his father and later overthrew him, establishing his rule over the cosmos. Zeus divided the world with his brothers, Poseidon and Hades, claiming the sky as his domain while they ruled the sea and the underworld. Known for his immense power, Zeus wielded the thunderbolt, crafted by the Cyclopes, as his signature weapon, capable of striking down his enemies. He was often depicted seated on a throne, holding a scepter or an eagle, his sacred animal, symbolizing his authority and connection to the heavens. Zeus was also the god of law, order, and justice, ensuring the balance of the universe and acting as a protector of oaths and hospitality.

Despite his role as a just ruler, Zeus was infamous for his numerous love affairs with both goddesses and mortals, fathering many important figures in Greek mythology, including Athena, Apollo, Artemis, Hermes, Perseus, and Hercules. His relationships often caused conflict, particularly with his wife, Hera, who frequently sought revenge on his lovers and illegitimate children. Worship of Zeus was widespread in ancient Greece, with grand temples like the Temple of Zeus at Olympia, where the Olympic Games were held in his honor. His name became synonymous with supreme power and authority, embodying both the benevolence and unpredictability of the divine. Zeus remains one of the most iconic figures in Greek mythology, representing the might and majesty of the gods.

In Roman mythology, Jupiter was the king of the gods, ruler of the sky, and god of thunder, serving as the Roman counterpart to the Greek god Zeus. As the son of Saturn (Cronus in Greek mythology) and Ops (Rhea), Jupiter overthrew his father to establish his dominion, dividing the cosmos with his brothers Neptune and Pluto, who ruled the sea and the underworld, respectively. Jupiter was the supreme deity of Roman religion, embodying authority, justice, and the natural order. He wielded the thunderbolt as his weapon, symbolizing his power to command the skies and punish wrongdoers. Often depicted with an eagle, his sacred animal, and holding a scepter, Jupiter was the protector of the Roman state and its laws, presiding over contracts, oaths, and treaties.

Jupiter was worshipped as part of the Capitoline Triad alongside Juno and Minerva, with his grand temple on Capitoline Hill serving as the center of Roman religious life. Festivals such as the Ludi Romani were held in his honor, featuring games, sacrifices, and celebrations to seek his favor and protection. Like his Greek counterpart, Jupiter was known for his numerous love affairs, fathering both mortal and divine offspring, which often caused intrigue and conflict in Roman myths. As the patron of victory and state power, Jupiter was deeply intertwined with Roman identity and governance, embodying the ideals of strength, leadership, and divine authority that defined Roman culture and religion.

Zeus and Jupiter, the Greek and Roman kings of the gods, are powerful figures representing authority, order, and the sky. Both deities share numerous similarities, including their roles as rulers of the pantheon, their association with thunder and lightning, and their positions as protectors of justice and law. Despite these shared attributes, Zeus and Jupiter also reflect the distinct cultural values and traditions of ancient Greece and Rome. Their influence on mythology, religion, and societal ideals continues to resonate in modern times, symbolizing leadership, power, and the connection between humanity and the divine.

In both Greek and Roman mythology, Zeus and Jupiter are supreme deities, ruling over the gods and mortals alike. They are often depicted wielding a thunderbolt, a symbol of their divine authority and power to enforce justice. Both gods are also associated with the sky, weather, and natural phenomena, reflecting their control over the elements. As arbiters of justice, Zeus and Jupiter maintained order in the cosmos, ensuring the balance between chaos and harmony. Their status as patriarchal figures extended beyond their divine roles, as they were also considered protectors of families, cities, and states.

Zeus, in Greek mythology, is the son of Cronus and Rhea and the youngest of the Olympian gods. After overthrowing his father Cronus, Zeus established himself as the ruler of Mount Olympus and divided the world with his brothers, Poseidon and Hades. Zeus's myths often highlight his complex personality, as he is depicted as both a wise and just ruler and a flawed figure prone to indulgence and infidelity. His numerous romantic liaisons with both goddesses and mortals resulted in a pantheon of offspring, many of whom became prominent figures in Greek mythology, such as Athena, Apollo, Artemis, and Heracles. Zeus was widely worshipped across Greece, with major sanctuaries at Olympia and Dodona. The Olympic Games, held in his honor, celebrated his role as a unifying figure and a symbol of physical and moral excellence.

Jupiter, the Roman counterpart to Zeus, retained many of his Greek attributes but was more closely tied to the political and civic life of Rome. As the chief deity of the Capitoline Triad, alongside Juno and Minerva, Jupiter was a central figure in Roman state religion. He was revered as Jupiter Optimus Maximus (Jupiter the Best and Greatest), a title that emphasized his role as a protector of the Roman state and its people. Unlike Zeus, whose myths often explored his personal flaws and relationships, Jupiter was portrayed as a more stoic and dignified figure, reflecting Roman ideals of discipline and authority. Temples dedicated to Jupiter, such as the Temple of Jupiter Optimus Maximus on the Capitoline Hill, served as centers of worship and political activity, reinforcing his connection to the governance and stability of Rome.

The influence of Zeus and Jupiter on their respective societies was profound. In ancient Greece, Zeus embodied the ideals of leadership, justice, and the interconnectedness of gods and mortals. His myths and worship inspired philosophical discussions about the nature of power and morality, as well as the human desire to understand the divine. In Rome, Jupiter's role as a protector of the state and a symbol of Roman supremacy underscored the importance of civic duty and the integration of religion and politics. His festivals and rituals reinforced the values of loyalty, discipline, and unity that were central to Roman identity.

In modern times, Zeus and Jupiter continue to be symbols of leadership, authority, and the mysteries of the cosmos. Zeus's mythology, with its themes of power, morality, and human flaws, remains a rich source of inspiration for literature, art, and popular culture. Jupiter, as the largest planet in the solar system, carries his name as a reflection of his grandeur and dominance, symbolizing humanity's enduring fascination with the heavens and the forces that govern the universe.

Zeus and Jupiter embody timeless themes of power, justice, and the relationship between mortals and the divine. Their myths and roles highlight the complexities of leadership and the responsibilities that come with great authority. From ancient temples to modern storytelling, these gods continue to inspire and illuminate the enduring human quest for understanding, order, and connection to the divine.

Manufactured by Amazon.ca
Acheson, AB